Edited by Konrad Hopkins and Ronald van Roekel

Cover by Craig Maclachlan

ROCKY SHORES:
An Anthology of Faroese Poetry

Compiled and Translated from the Faroese and the Danish
(William Heinesen), and with an Introduction and
Notes on the Poems

by

George Johnston

With Biographical Notes and a Selected Bibliography

't Kan verkeeren.
('Things can change.')

— G.A. Bredero

A RonKon Paperback
WILFION BOOKS, PUBLISHERS
Paisley, Scotland
1981

ISBN 0 905075 10 2

Printed by

            Alexander Speirs,
            54 Ewing Street,
            Rutherglen,
            Glasgow,
            Scotland, U.K.

First published in Great Britain by

            Wilfion Books, Publishers
            12 Townhead Terrace,
            Paisley, Renfrewshire PA1 2AX,
            Scotland, U.K.

ACKNOWLEDGEMENTS

Poems in this anthology have previously appeared, in English translation by George Johnston, in the following magazines:

Poetry (Chicago): William Heinesen, 'Rain in Leningrad'; Karsten Hoydal, 'White Night', 'Stones'; Christian Matras, 'The Company of the Blind', 'So Deep, So Deep';

Quarry (Canada): Karsten Hoydal, 'To Ruth', 'White Sand'; Christian Matras, 'The Sheltering Wall', 'Weather Troll';

Tamarack Review (Canada): Christian Matras, 'Far Off the Sea';

Anthos (Ottawa) : William Heinesen, 'A Summer's Day'; Christian Matras, 'Milk Women'; Steinbjørn B. Jacobsen, 'Sun Bait';

Inscape (Ottawa): Steinbjørn B. Jacobsen, 'A Summer Moment', 'Yolk';

Trends (Scotland): William Heinesen, 'Winter Lights Its Flame on Our Mountains', 'The Dark Talks to a Blossoming Bush', 'Stone Girl'; Karsten Hoydal, 'White Sand', 'Out from the Rocky Shore', 'The Drop'; Christian Matras, 'We Two on the Still Strand', 'Now Is Our Life like a Lantern Light', 'Vithoy'.

**UNESCO COLLECTION
OF REPRESENTATIVE WORKS
EUROPEAN SERIES**

This book has been accepted in the European Series of the Translations Collection of the United Nations Educational, Scientific and Cultural Organization (Unesco).

PUBLISHERS' NOTE

Wilfion Books was established in 1975 to commemorate William Sharp/Fiona Macleod (known privately to his wife and first cousin, Elizabeth A. Sharp, as 'Wilfion'), a man of letters who was born in Paisley, Scotland, in 1855.

His literary output was enormous, consisting of novels, short stories, biographies, plays, collections of poetry, edited volumes of other authors' writings, works of art history, boys' adventure tales, and countless articles, reviews, and essays of art and literary criticism. About half his total production was issued under his own name, while the rest was published under the pseudonym Fiona Macleod; and as Fiona Macleod, whose poems, tales, romances, and plays had Celtic legends and folk-lore as their subjects, Sharp, who was never publicly identified with Fiona Macleod during his lifetime, became the leading light in the Celtic Revival in Scotland in the late 19th century.

A Scot by birth, he was a Scandinavian by inheritance from his mother. His maternal grandfather, the Swedish Vice Consul at Glasgow, was of Swedish descent: and William resembled him in appearance, being tall, with a 'Scandinavian physique', and fair-complexioned. Mrs. Sharp wrote of him in her *Memoir*: 'The blend of nationalities in him, slight though the Swedish strain was, produced a double strain. He was, in the words of a friend, a Viking in build, a Scandinavian in cast of mind, a Celt in heart and spirit.'

When he was a boy in Paisley, he listened with rapt attention to the stories his Highland nurse, Barbara, told him about '. . . the heroes of the old Celtic Sagas, . . . the daring exploits of the Viking rovers and Highland chieftains', and in his childhood games ' . . . he delighted in being the adventurous warrior or marauding Viking' (quoted from Mrs. Sharp's *Memoir*, p. 5). Years later, he put these stories and games to literary use in a boys' adventure serial called *The Last of the Vikings*, which was published in *The Young Folks' Paper*.

Just as he was divided in his personality between the masculine Sharp and the feminine Macleod, so was he divided in his geographical preferences. On the one hand, like many other British writers, he yearned for the 'beautiful, living, pulsing

South' (as far South as Sicily, where he died in 1905 and was buried under a Celtic cross in the shadow of Mt. Etna); on the other hand, he was in his imagination drawn to the North, to '... the dark mountains and the wild, beautiful Scandinavian seas', as he wrote in his short story 'Fröken Bergliot', about a Norwegian woman, 'a northern soul', living in isolation in Italy and longing for her Nordic home. In the same story, a young Sharp-like painter cries out, ' "Oh, for the breath of the Blue Fiord!" '

In literature, too, his passions were divided between South and North. As a critic, he studied and wrote about a number of foreign literatures, Italian, French and Provençal among them; but he also wrote a long scholarly article on 'Icelandic Literature: The Sagas (Ninth to Thirteenth Century)', and among the references he listed were works by F. York Powell, whose English version of *The Faereyinga Saga* was published in 1896; and he was acquainted with William Morris, who had visited the Faroe Islands and Iceland in 1871 and was a pioneer in translating the Icelandic Sagas into English.

Furthermore, Sharp was familiar with the plays of Ibsen, probably those translated by his fellow Scotsman, William Archer, in the late 1880s and in the 1890s. (Sharp's first cousin and brother-in-law, R. Farquharson Sharp, Keeper of Printed Books at the British Museum, also translated Ibsen's plays in four series and Bjørnson's plays in two series, in the early years of the 20th century, but after Sharp's death.) However, Sharp/Macleod did not find Ibsen's social realism congenial, favouring instead the impressionistic closet dramas of Maurice Maeterlinck. In the preface to 'her' own play of this type, *The House of Usna*, Fiona Macleod declared: 'The theatre of Ibsen, and all it stands for, is become outworn as a compelling influence. Its inherent tendency to demonstrate intellectually from a series of incontrovertible material facts is not adequate to those who would see in the drama the means to demonstrate symbolically from a sequence of intuitive perception.' Nevertheless, as Professor Flavia Alaya points out in her biography of Sharp (1970), Ibsen's *Rosmersholm* (1886) has enough similarities to Sharp's novel *The Children of To-morrow* (1889) to suggest that perhaps Sharp had been influenced by the sexual and social concepts in Ibsen's play.

Our motto, *'t Kan verkeeren* ('Things can change'), was originated in the play, *Griane* (1612), by the Dutch poet and dramatist, Gerbrand Adriaenszoon Bredero (1585-1618). It became his personal motto, inscribed on many of his private letters, and we have adopted it as our own to remember him as well, because of our associations with the Netherlands. Our emblem, the *crux aeterna*, composed of a heart enclosing the cross and surmounted by the sign of infinity, represents the universality and eternality of love and the spirit.

Mr. John Button of The Thule Press, Stornoway, Isle of Lewis, Scotland, first introduced us to Faroese literature, and we are grateful to him for his encouragement and sympathetic interest in our plan to publish an anthology of Faroese poetry in English translation.

In realising our plan, we have had the full co-operation of Professor George Johnston, the compiler and translator of *Rocky Shores*, and of Mr. Karsten Hoydal, former Chairman of the Faroese Authors' Society, who first brought to our notice the existence of Professor Johnston's translations. Their helpful suggestions and patient counsel have guided us in everything relating to this anthology, from choosing the title to assembling the Selected Bibliography, for which Dr. John F. West has kindly given us leave to extract some entries from the 'English Bibliography' in his *Faroe: The Emergence of a Nation* (1972). To these three gentlemen we offer our sincerest thanks.

Nor can we forget to acknowledge the invaluable assistance and perseverance of Mr. Lionel Izod and Mr. Moënis Taha-Hussein, both of the Literature Division of Unesco, in supporting us towards the eventual publication of this present anthology.

Finally, we must acknowledge our debt of gratitude to the nine poets themselves, for without their generous contributions the publication of *Rocky Shores: An Anthology of Faroese Poetry* would not have been possible at all.

— Konrad Hopkins and Ronald van Roekel

Paisley/Amsterdam,
23 December 1980

To
Hans and Else Bekker-Nielsen

CONTENTS

INTRODUCTION

by

George Johnston

The Faroes are a small archipelago in the North Atlantic, between Shetland and Iceland, consisting of eighteen islands, most of them inhabited. They stretch approximately a hundred and thirteen kilometers from north to south and seventy-five from east to west. Their population in 1966 was thirty-seven thousand and it has increased since then to perhaps forty-four thousand. Many Faroese also live in Denmark, of which country the islands are a dependency, though they run most of their own affairs and have achieved something very near to independence.

They were settled in the ninth century, during the great Viking expansion, by Norwegians, who were at the same time settling Iceland, Shetland, Orkney, the British Isles and Greenland. The language of these settlers was West Norse, and it has survived in Iceland and the Faroes, and is at present being revived from local dialects in Norway. Modern Icelandic has hardly changed from the language of these first settlers. Faroese, however, has been less conservative and has lost most of its inflections, though its vocabulary has remained pure. Icelandic has one of the most impressive literary traditions in Europe; in it are preserved the greatest portion of all the heroic writings of the German peoples. Faroese has had no written literature until the twentieth century. It has persisted, miraculously, as the language spoken by a handful of people, who preserved their cultural identity and vitality, without political independence, through hard centuries, assailed by plague, famine and piracy. During the Second World War these people played a heroic part, though their country was technically neutral. When the Nazis occupied Denmark and Norway the British forces occupied the Faroes, who suffered terrible losses in men to German air and submarine attack, as fishermen, supplying the United Kingdom, and as merchant seamen in the Allied merchant fleet.

ii

Faroese is both an old and a new language. It has a large and varied oral 'literature' consisting of ballads, which are still sung and danced to in the islands, much as they have been all down through the centuries, since the medieval round dance. The ballads were collected by the Faroese scholar V.U. Hammershaimb in 1891 and published with a glossary in Danish. This was an important landmark in the establishment of Faroese as a literary language, though the same scholar had already published, in 1846, a Faroese orthography founded on etymological principles, and this was used in the writing of poetry, particularly by Faroese students in Copenhagen, from 1876. Danish had been, since the seventeenth century, the official language of the country, and it is only within living memory that sermons have been preached and school-children taught in Faroese.

Faroese writers are all modern. They know the ballads but hardly seem to be influenced by them. Their language is somewhat archaic in spelling, but modern in its outlook and forms. Their readers are a tiny group, close-knit and full of affection for their community and homeland. They are not provincial in spite of the village quality of much of their life, and their innocence, as yet, of tourists; many Faroese are widely travelled and sophisticated, and their domestic arrangements, their kitchens, for instance, are as modern as one sees in Copenhagen or Stockholm.

The mass media have hardly affected this new-old language. Advertising means little in such a community, and a recent plebiscite rejected television. The words available to the poets seem forthright and unaffectedly lyrical. Much of their poetry is written in the unrhymed, more or less unmeasured forms that we think of as having come to English poetry through Ezra Pound. There has been little interest in experimentation among them, but on the other hand they have almost altogether given up the traditional rhymed forms. Their poetry is middle-of-the-road modern and intelligible; in mood it is mainly lyrical.

Christian Matras is, in my opinion, the foremost of the poets now writing in Faroese. He was born in 1900 and grew up in the parsonage of Viðareiði, the village at the northernmost tip of the islands. When he was a child, fishing was not yet the industrial activity it has become for the Faroese, so that the fishing boat, whose safe homecoming he celebrates in 'Knee-Rocking Song' (p. 9), was a rowing boat, and the catch it brought in was mainly for local consumption; its crew were farmers and shepherds first, and fishermen when they could be. As a child he knew the centuries-old life and economy of the islands, which has since become radically modern and dependent on a world economy, especially since the Second World War. His nostalgia for the islands, which is characteristic of all the poets, whether they are at home or abroad, is grounded in his first-hand experience of the old life during its dying years. He also remembered the idioms of his village, and older turns of speech. Sometimes these lay hidden deep in his memory for many years, and could not be called up, but came to the surface in their own time. He explained his poem 'Far off the Sea' (p. 14) one morning and took much of the morning to do so, and said that the phrase that names the mysterious loud noise the sea sometimes makes inland, during a stillness, came to him after forty years; meanwhile the poem remained unfinished. He has said that poetry is his first love, but this is inseparable from his other great interest, language, specifically his beloved Faroese. His scholarly work in this field is of international importance, and he is recognised internationally. He has compiled, with M.A. Jacobsen, the first and as yet only modern Faroese dictionary, excluding Hammershaimb's glossary.

Christian Matras is the most traditional of the poets in this anthology. Many of his stanzas are modelled on the hymns of the Danish hymn writer, Thomas Kingo. His rhythms are subtle and sure, and his metres, whether rhymed and counted or not, are simple. A poet's rhythm can be heard more or less steadily in everything he or she writes, regardless of the particular meter or verse form. If he or she writes prose it will be heard in that as well. His greatness as a poet can be heard in Christian Matras's rhythm, which is steady in all his work, and also in the pace of his speech. It is possible to imagine an influence on his language of the rhythms of the sea, which were in his ears day and night throughout his childhood. But one is also aware, in talking with him, of an evenness of temper and motion that seems to belong to his nature. The mood of his poetry is lyrical; there is hardly a trace of satire or opinion in it, but it shows the fine enjoyment of the comic and strange which he shares with other Faroese poets, notably his great contemporary, William Heinesen.

William Heinesen grew up in Tórshavn, where the first language he spoke, his mother tongue, was Danish. He has therefore written in Danish, and his poetry differs somewhat in character from the rest in this anthology. One is tempted to suggest that Danish is a more cosmopolitan and sophisticated language than Faroese because of its more cosmopolitan history, but this could be no better than conjecture. Heinesen himself is not more cosmopolitan than his fellow-writers, many of whom have as wide-ranging experience of the world as he has.

He is also a novelist, whose novels are widely known and admired, particularly in Scandinavia. And he is a painter and graphic artist and a musician and composer. The energy and variety of his gifts are apparent in his poetry, in the vitality of his response to life, his compassion, his stoicism, his awareness of the tragic and inexorable, and his love of the comic. He is an older man with an impressive career, chiefly as a novelist, behind him: he was born in 1900, the same year as Christian Matras and Jørgen-Frantz Jacobsen, and a year before Heðin Brú. These four, two writing in Faroese — Christian Matras and Heðin Brú — and the other two in Danish, are recognised as great literary figures at home and elsewhere in Scandinavia, and their works will have an assured place in world literature.

One might say of Karsten Hoydal that he is philosophical, and that philosophical statements come to the fore sometimes in his poetry, as though to claim special attention. But, though he has written short stories and critical prose, he is essentially a poet, with a lyrical gift. His breath has a deep fetch and will carry his thought over long phrases. In the content of his poems this expresses itself in a philosophical optimism, which is in the grain of his nature. It sometimes comes to the surface in the form of declarations, but mostly it affects us as a sweetness in his lyrical poems, because it is not an easy optimism, but a manly acceptance of what life has to offer. He has been a practical man, trained in fish processing and marketing, and he has served his country in the department of its vital fishing industry. He has been an administrator and elected representative in the Faroese government, and he has served with the FAO abroad in Ecuador as a fisheries expert.

Regin Dahl is a personal kind of poet, with an eye for small dramas that involve himself or those around him. The mood evoked by these dramas is usually lyrical, though there may be satirical or social comment in them as well, and an occasional touch of black singles out his poetry from the rest. He has written explicitly religious poems, though not orthodox. Nostalgia for the islands is no less strong in him than in the others, but it is more clearly from self-imposed exile. He has been a reader in Gyldendal's publishing house in Copenhagen for many years.

What little experimental poetry one knows of in Faroese has all been written by Steinbjørn Jacobsen. He is a younger man than any of the preceding, with most of his writing career still before him, but old enough to have established a firm reputation, and to have written a varied body of work, in prose (including children's books and plays) and poetry. He too is essentially a poet and like Christian Matras he has an interest in words for their own sakes. He is a man of impulsive energies and affections, and his impatience can be felt in some of his verse, whose poetic quality is nevertheless kept by his vision. This vision can be recognised in every part of his varied life. He has a young family, and his house seems full of the presence of children. He is interested in all the arts, and also in skin-diving; he is a nationalist and principal of the Faroese Folk High School. Except for Christian Matras he is the most intensely Faroese of the poets, and the impulsiveness of his pace makes an interesting foil to Christian Matras's steadiness.

Guðrið Helmsdal is the most personal of the poets. She writes of her own loves and fears and pleasures, clearly and open-heartedly, and in unsophisticated modern verse forms.

There is no irony or impatience in her statements, which seem therefore candid and pure in feeling. Rói Patursson, by contrast, is public in his concerns and socially conscious in his statements. Faroese economy has been simple and non-industrial, except insofar as its fishing techniques are industrial, and its society is as near classless and rural as can be. There are no cities: Tórshavn, the capital, has a population of about fourteen thousand. The urban predicaments and attitudes in Rói Patursson's poetry belong to Copenhagen, and these make him, in many respects, the most cosmopolitan of the poets. His images and rhythms are strong, but one sometimes feels more potentiality than realisation in them, as yet. Perhaps Faroese has not got the idioms for everything he wants to say. Steinbjørn Jacobsen and Karsten Hoydal have also written socially conscious poems, but these have not seemed close to the centre of their concerns.

Alexandur Kristiansen is a young school-teacher in the village of Fuglafjørdur, where he was born. He has already published six collections of poetry, and he writes in a style that seems easy and fluent, but also deft and rather sophisticated. There is a vein of wry and often playful surrealism in his writing, and not so much nostalgia as in many of the other poets. He and Heðin M. Klein are the youngest represented in this anthology. Klein chooses disciplined, almost tight-lipped forms, and his meanings are concentrated in symbolic language. His rhythms are not so much varied or graceful as strong, and they are full of promise.

There are other young and promising poets and a few fine older poets, two or three of a generation previous to any representated in this collection. It cannot pretend to be a comprehensive anthology; it is, however, representative of a small, self-contained and unusual tradition of twentieth-century poetry.

ROCKY SHORES:

An Anthology of Faroese Poetry

CHRISTIAN MATRAS was born in 1900 in the northern-most village in the Islands, Viðareiði, on the island of Viðoy, and grew up in the rectory there. His early schooling was in the village, and from there he went to Tórshavn and then proceeded to gymnasium at Sorø, Denmark, and to the university at Copenhagen. He studied Nordic philology, obtaining a master's degree in 1928 and a doctor's degree in 1933. He lectured in Copenhagen University and was there during the Second World War. Since 1965 he has been professor of Faroese language and culture and director of language studies in the Faroese Academy (Fróðskaparsetur) in Tórshavn.

His honours, as a philological scholar, have been many, at home in Scandinavia and in the wider world of learning. The most important of his scholarly publications is his Faroese-Danish dictionary, which he compiled with the assistance of the librarian, M.A. Jacobsen. It is the first and only such dictionary (except for Hammershaimb's Glossary) and a supplement to it was recently issued, under his direction, by Jóhan Hendrik Winther Poulsen.

His collections of poetry include *Grátt, kátt og hátt* (an untranslatable word-play, but roughly Gray, Bright and Solemn), 1926; *Heimur og Heima* (the World and Home), 1933; *Úr leikum og loyndum* (From Open Life and Secret), 1940; a selection called simply *Yrkingar* (Poems), 1965; and *Á hellu eg stóð* (On the Rock-strand I Stood), 1972. In 1975 his collected poems and translations were published under the title *Leikur og Loynd* (Open and Secret); and in the same year a new collection, *Av Viðareiði/Fólk í huganum* (From Viðareiði/Folk of My Heart) came out. In 1978 a small collection of poems, *Úr sjón og úr minni, ørindi* (Seen and Remembered, Verse), appeared.

Other books include translations and critical works. The former are of Thomas Kingo's hymns, 1939; of Robert Burns' *Poems*, 1945; of William Heinesen's *Níggju yrkingar* (Nine Poems), 1970; and of his old friend Jørgen-Frantz Jacobsen's novel *Barbara* from Danish into Faroese, called *Barba og Harra Pál*, 1972. Among the latter are *Føroysk bókmentasøga*

(Faroese Literary History), 1935; *Glydendals Julebog: Jørgen-Frantz Jacobsen*, 1941; and *Nøkur mentafólk, greinir og róður* (Some Cultural Figures, Articles and Lectures), 1973.

His poems have been translated into Nynorsk, Danish, Swedish, Serbo-Croatian, and English.

WE TWO ON THE STILL STRAND

It was in a world of fair-weather fog
the islands out there had gone
and soft small waves came back and forth to shore
they hardly wanted to break.
We two alone on the foreshore
waded quietly out
and began to play with the cool wavelets quietly,
yes, with the whole unspoiled world
that God had made in the first days.

NOW IS OUR LIFE LIKE A LANTERN LIGHT

Night swells on the land,
severs the last nerve strand
that bound day to earth.
Dark clings on the ledge,
fills chasm and cleft ridge
and village street and firth.

Mold-dark moon dark closes in.
All that in daylight might be seen
goes under swart night.
Now life is a lantern beam
that winks round the stable's gloom
and sheds a homely light.

THE SHELTERING WALL

The rock-point stands out below.
Cliff darkens in the old wound.
Juts of gray rock reach into the air above.

Blue water against the cliff.
Cold sea whitens
in on dim stones.

These were walls against the sea set
and north storm.
Turf hung down from rock-jut.
Boulders lay on the bottom.

Cliff crumbled where it stood,
loosed the rock-slip —
skerry and rock-fall stay as giant grounds.

Cliff-rag and rock-glut are now the land's defense.
Sucking and licking tide and surf
wear ancient stone.

VITHOY

Sail, island, forth from the fog, you are a ship now
with peaks for masts;
you set your course into the great world
with your pastures and mountain crests.

Your prow breaks water at Enniberg,
white water at Nanestang.
Always you sail foremost of the fleet
where currents are running strong.

We look up to the masthead,
ridges and peaks show bright.
Now it clears down to the rock strand
and homely fields take light.

And circling birds fore and aft
they liven up scree and sward.
And folk and flocks and curlew cries
are the dear freight on board.

WINTER

Earth tilts again, her axis alters
— under dark rafters the north half-world shelters.

Under heaven's roof frost demons frolic
and in the troll night the moon god makes magic.

Wide over sea wastes sea dragons chase
— stiff run the rivers like troll piss.

Chasms all plug with blind dumb trolls
— giants lunge through the land, that come from the fells.

WEATHER TROLL

Now it is winter and almost night
and the troll sits and cards batt
in some stone that the winds hug
and sucks man-marrow and chews rag.

And the troll cards and the troll cards
and heaps up gray stuff, yards and yards;
wind lays about and slings troll-gray
and has a feed that is all coal-gray.

And man sleeps and never kens
that the wind steps a spooky dance
and whirls troll-gray everywhere;
night fled away, she died of fear.

And day took over in troll-gray
sure in the light he knew the way,
but the sun grinned a rueful grin,
she was too old to be taken in.

And the sun flags as day wears
for the airts are gray all wheres,
and the troll cards and the troll cards
and heaps more gray stuff, yards and yards.

KNEE-ROCKING SONG

They row, they row, in through the sound.
Outside they hand-lined, caught a few pound.
They steer, they steer, in under the ness,
then along the shore line, — oars keep pace.
Now a call from the look-out: 'They come!'

They quicken, they quicken, weary men in the boat,
make straight for the landing, where it is called 'Wet'.
Young ones, young ones, creep down the banks,
old chaps after them, hopping on bent shanks,
and women with hot drink in wrapped bottles.

Back-row, back-row these cunning men to shore.
Few words in their mouths, bad luck to say more.
They unship, unship fish heaps on the stones.
Down from the rock-jut the last gaffer groans.
Now they haul the boat up on the launch.

They banter, they banter about weather and catch.
Safe up on land at last. Give a hand each
for the long haul, long haul to the boat-house in the banks.
Women make their ways home, giving inward thanks
that the dear freight is safe returned once more.

They saunter, they saunter back home again.
Every rock and tuft of grass seem to know the men.
Beyond the path, beyond the path streams run in the ghylls.
It is all kind and homey, ducks in the pools.
Doors creak again in the houses.

MILK WOMEN

Milk women come now south from the leaze,
buckets at their backs, weariness in their knees.
Milk slops in the wood, heather on the hill
pricks under foot, and gravel in the ghyll.
Home lies the little one and sleeps.

Milk women come now south to the bourns,
goose-file they come, like hill marker-cairns
that started to walk when light left the heaths.
Gates open for them and wide village paths.
Home lies the little one and sleeps.

Milk women in the lanes, heavily they step.
Cats at home here, watch for their drop,
flatten in the grass till milk women come,
night at their backs and buckets to the brim.
Home lies the little one and sleeps.

THE COMPANY OF THE BLIND

On into the darkness
the blind go
wherever whim takes them
each every way.
None remembers the why,
only the going —
it is the blind company
and its way is long.

Some tire early
and give up,
others think the journey
without worth or hope,
only follow the stream
undesiring
not understanding, dream-
walking.

Then in some blessed time
what's wonderful
opens the blind eye,
gives life and will,
moments remembered
of bright weather
that bring long and sundered
paths together.

On into blindness again
all go

wherever whim leads them
each every way.

None remembers the why
only the going —
it is the blind company
and its way is long.

SO DEEP, SO DEEP

Into my soul so deep, so deep was planted
a joy, whatever it was, mortal, granted —
as quickly buried under remembered stuff;
the whole of life in a swift second of life.

Under the heavy weight of day by day
it grew as something living, a seed of joy —
at a touch of memory it will swell,
this joy, a second of life, earthed in the soul.

FAR OFF THE SEA

Softly falls the night
and children are in the field below the fences.
They run for the haybarn door
whose shrunk boards leak
sweetness into the dusk.

Far off the sea whets his roar
in the hushed night between the hills.

WILLIAM HEINESEN was born in Tórshavn in 1900. Most widely-known of the poets in this anthology, and a frequent nominee for the Nobel Prize in Literature, he has published short stories and novels as well as poems, and he is also a composer and a painter. His stories, novels and poems are written in Danish, but he has also written critical articles in Faroese.

His short stories appear in two collections, *Det fortryllede lys* and *Gamaliels besættelse* his novels are *Blæsende gry*, *De fortabte spillemaend* (translated into English by Erik Friis as *The Lost Musicians*), *Noatun* (translated into English by Jan Noble as *Niels Peter*), *Den sorte gryde* and *Det gode håb*. *Fortællinger fra Thorshavn* is a collection of reminiscences and stories about Tórshavn and *Det dyrebare liv* is an edition he made of some letters of his good friend, the Faroese novelist, Jørgen-Frantz Jacobsen. He also put Jacobsen's last manuscript into publishable shape as the novel *Barbara* after Jacobsen's early death. This novel achieved immediate and lasting fame in Scandinavia, and an English translation by Estrid Bannister was published by Penguin.

William Heinesen has published seven collections of poetry: *Arktiske elegier og andre digte* (Arctic Elegies and Other Poems), 1921; *Høbjergning ved havet* (Haymaking by the Sea), 1924; *Sange mod vårdybet* (Songs for the Depth of Spring), 1927; *Stjernerne vågner* (The Stars Wake Up), 1927; *Den dunkle sol* (The Dark Sun), 1936; *Hymne og harmsang* (Hymns and Songs of Wrath),1961; and *Panorama med regnbue* (Panorama with Rainbow), 1972. *Digte i Udvalg* (Selected Poems) appeared in 1955.

Three other books should be mentioned: *Kur mod onde Ånder*, 1967; *Don Juan fra Tranhuset*, 1970; and *Tårnet ved Verdens Ende*, 1976. He has also written the text for a book of photographs of the Islands by Gérard Franceschi called, in the English version, *The Faroe Islands, the Magic Islands*, 1971.

His work has been written about in English by Hedin Brønner in his book *Three Faroese Novelists*, 1973, and in an article, 'William Heinesen: Faroese Writer — Danish Pen', in *The*

American-Scandinavian Review. W. Glyn Jones is the author of a monograph, *William Heinesen,* in Twayne's World Authors Series, and of two articles in English:'*Noatun* and the Collective Novel' in *Scandinavian Studies,* 1969, and 'William Heinesen and the Myth of Conflict' in *Scandinavica,* 1970. For further information on these publications in English, see the Selected Bibliography.

WINTER LIGHTS ITS FLAME ON OUR MOUNTAINS

Winter lights its flame on our mountains.
Now come the still opal-gray days
and the troll-filled early gloaming
with the new moon's red knife-edge on the horizon
and the showery days
with their daybreak's polychrome quarry skies
and the storm-gray days when the ocean blossoms.
Now the playful Northern Lights come back
and the stately constellations
and the roadway's crazy sparkling ice crystals.

Now you come too
my dead friends
deeply and constantly missed,
and warm your hands by my winter fire.
See, your favourite food and drink is on the table
and the music you loved
sounds through the room.
Then your voices too come to life
your glad laughter
your wondering cry
when the majestic Andromeda nebula's million-year-old light
emerges into the telescope's field at the open window
and lets our mortal eyes gather
a precious drop of eternity.

THE DARK TALKS TO A BLOSSOMING BUSH

I am the dark.
Do you feel my cheek against you?
Do you feel my black mouth against your red?

Yes, you are the dark and you make me afraid.
You are night and eternity.
I am aware of your cold breath.
You are death.
You want me to wither.
I so much want to live and blossom.

I am the dark.
I love you.
I want you to wither.
Blossom and wither.
Wither and grow up again with your flowers.
Again and again wither and grow up again.

I am the night. Death. Eternity.
I love you.
I would die if you were not
and did not stand here and wait for me
with your perishable flowers' anxious flame.
With your living brother-and-sisterhood
of warm red kiss
deep in my lone black heart.

THE DISMAL WOODS

No, this is no station, here —
it is the middle of a deep woods.
The locomotive groans once or twice
and then settles down and becomes still,
as though it stood with flaring nostrils
and black, wild eyes
and breathed the panic night air.

We have halted somewhere in Germany's dark heart.
Compartment windows open
and here and there in the steamy coach
faces come in sight.
A wind blows through the wood,
and between the black treetops can be seen in the
        vertiginous dark throat of the heavens
Orion's terrifying shape.

The stillness is at the same time frightening and romantic —
one begins to think of train wrecks
and about the Erl King
and about nocturnal, surging Beethoven Sonatas
music of eternity and the heart's disquiet,
and one feels strangely, fatally put out of the game.

The woods and loneliness do violence to the Continental Express!
The passengers begin to grumble a little
and talk of disorganisation and obsolete rolling stock,
forget in their naiveté
that we live in subversiveness's obscure times,

technology's and destruction's paradoxical century.
(And are naturally no longer willing to listen to the
                              unfathomable murmur
from the ancient Eichendorf trees!)

But at last we get moving again,
this little romantic intermezzo is over,
the locomotive snorts lustfully
and the string of coaches rattles into stride
and penetrates in triumph the dismal woods.

FORTUNA

Full moon climbs from the sea
red as a pepper —
childhood's old adventure moon,
dream and myth laden,
a moist, splendid orb
where seas break on strange coasts
in ecstatic and unheard-of loneliness.

There comes a small ship sailing
under tanned murky sails.
Sweetly it creaks in its timbers
and taut drawn rigging.
A weathered and bearded salt
stands silent by the wheel.

But see: if it is not *Fortuna*!
But surely, it is *Fortuna*!
the dear old sloop
that we played aboard as boys
on uncharted dream voyages
while she lay safely tied
to her moorings in Tórshavn's harbour!
Fortuna with her dusky sails!
Fortuna with her stink of tar and pitch
and sun-parched manilla!
Now sails she here by the moon!

But though we know every plank
aboard that good old dream ship

and know the old man's face
it is only with fearful forebodings
that we come aboard
and take on the voyage.

We greet him: good evening, Sinbad!
He answers with a wry smile
and gives a seaman's stare
out into the sky, and the future.

The deck is wet with fog.
The air is misty and soft.
Mist-sea opens its arms.
So it was, when we as children
one misty endless day
leaned out the gable window
blowing bubbles
and were tickled down to our footsoles
as we sent rainbow orbs
out into hungry space.

But mark: a bewitching odour
turns us quickly in.
We are nearing *Nectar-sea*
and now we remember with sudden poignancy
that moment when we first
were made a present of oranges!
O magic sectioned fruit
with the taste of paradise,

sumptuous
with a pungent barbaric hint
of a new, palpable, sexual activity.

The odour takes hold and becomes threatening:
Generation-sea has opened
in quiet, sun-quivering power.
A demonic sargasso sea
with drifting algae islands
and fleets of bobbing medusas
and a damp as from gorgon weed hair
and slippery fish skins.
Here is no place to be.
It was like this often
on great petrified summer afternoons:
majestic stillness
but full of threat
and lurking angst.
Medusa eyes in the deep!

The old one at the wheel stares
far out with expert eye
where the waves roll green and wild:
now comes the *Danger-sea*.
Surf seethes and roars
with the sound of long knives whetting
and for all the sun-filled sky
all at once it is cold.

Yes, just this way it came,
the first hard grief:
with power and filled with light,
spellbound iridescent sunlight,
torturing light, heartless.
Here you go from me, brother,
lost in your first youth,
betrayed by these waves
that have neither reason nor mercy.
Your bright boy's face
at once shaken and knowing —
now to and fro in the foam.

The plank joints are creaking.
It thunders in mainsail and jib.
Wild dissonances sound
from the rigging's dark harp:
now comes the *Stormfilled-sea*.
Here! says the old skipper
and puts my hand on the wheel.
His face is haggard and weary.
His look is without pardon:

Now it is your turn — hallo!
Now it is your dog watch.

A SUMMER'S DAY

The whole day long
sang the sun.

Early in the morning
when it broke through the fog
epic and gnomic verses
from heroic ages,
      'Light flashes break from the fire mountain.'
Then crowed the cock.

Then towards noon-day
when the clover scent was strongest
mighty green hymns
of the world's splendid ordinariness.
      'A lovely and joyful summertime.'
Then cackled the hens.

Later in the afternoon
when ranunculus and ragged robin
smiling put their heads together
jocular verses
about love-life's astonishing naturalness.
      'The monks walk in the meadow.'
Then the children gave a cheer.

At last in the evening
when ocean grew dark in Earth's shadow
soft deep chorales
of every beloved thing's natural short-livedness.

'An eye-blink and the time is past
    of our breath in this place of dust.'
Then the slow-moving blue-bottle mused
and polished his glasses
and stared long but in vain
into space.

But the sun laughed knowingly
before he crept into his rosy eiderdown
and sang at last a song of the best
that tells of eternity's jovial rotundity.
        'You are lucky and happy all right
        Heaven will have you tonight.'
Then along came the midges on the wing
and busily wove their airy evening webs
of oblivion and nothing.

PAUSE

North behind the dark sky-line
heaven is full of the rosiest happiness
and most priceless humour.
It knows nothing of us dying
nevertheless
without us all this show would be the merest stuff
for nobody's eye.

PAUSE

All the humble flowers
on my late life-day's roadside
dance very quietly
in the magic eventide
arm in arm
hand in hand
so aching and beautiful a spirit dance.

RAIN IN LENINGRAD

It rains in the gray-light evening
over mirror-wet streets
over the bay and the dim river.
Quietly the grass trembles on the graves of the dead
under the steady rain.

Everywhere in the falling wetness
stand young leafy trees
planted by the city folk
after war's end and victory
and bitter loss.
Every man every woman every child,
their hope's green tree.

In the Winter Palace there is a hall
of pure gold.
Today it was full of silent, staring people.
This evening only the gold is at home
behind rain-wet panes in the dark halls.

STONE GIRL

Into the dusk she rises
from the gravel-covered square,
wet in the evening breezes

as if she had come forth
out of a deep in the land
on to some homely strand.

And she stands there — a guest
from a kingdom far and wild,
yet just a girl child,

a mystery in stone
yet simple and mild
as a leaf on a vine.

An eye-blink brings together
the friendly and the frightening,
a silent, eerie meeting.

Then on comes the night.
Now she is a priestess
of no human rite.

She stands the morning after
among the playing children
like any Earth's daughter.

CHILD'S DRAWING

Tower in the west
stands in the great ocean.
Surf roars.
Birds scream.
A ship sails by and hoots:
ohoy, oho.
    Tower in the west is called 'Hoyaho'.

Tower in the east
stands in a black forest.
Wolves howl: ulayula ulaloya.
Tower in the east has beard and hair.
It shows its teeth like a dog.
It is called 'Voyavoya'.

Tower in the south
pokes up into the clouds.
It is full of faces
and eyes and mouths
and hear how it sings: amen, amen!
    Tower in the south is called 'Amen-amen'.

Tower in the north is called Rok.
It stands on the mountain Rokkebok.
It has a peep-hole and a hoisting block.
That's enough talk.

A BALLAD OF OLD KNIGHTS

We have come a long way over the heath
all we older time men
on our night-dark horses.
It is not so long again
     till cockcrow
     till cockcrow

We have come far over the rough river
all we older time men.
We have come far up out of the deep valley
where the river roars its sorrowful roar
     its twilight roar
     before cockcrow.

Then we ride into your town
all we older time men
     the new town
     the young town
where the gables all shine
in trustworthy dawn again.

     Hark, the first cockcrow!

We stay only a short while in your town.
all we older time men.
Then we ride into the sunrise
never, never more
to turn back again.
     Because now the world is new

and all the cocks are crowing
in the wild sky.

DEDICATION

Slowly darkens
March evening's frost-clear sky.
Sun has gone down.
Stars light up behind the black fells.
Low in the east over the horizon
can be felt the new moon's airy
spiderweb-fine sickle.

All the roads and paths that I have gone!
Now there is only one back,
the last wild path
over the dusking sea and into the dark.
That shall I walk with thanks in my heart.

That shall I walk
and think with tenderness of you
who are yet young on the earth —
you who have the sunset
and your longing and ache.
You who have evening star and your hope.
You who have new moon and your love.

KARSTEN HOYDAL was born in Tórshavn in 1912, and grew up in an adjacent village. He was educated in agronomy in Copenhagen and went on to make a special study of the fishing industry. During the Second World War he worked in the research laboratories of the Danish ministry of fisheries in Copenhagen. He became director of the Faroese fisheries technical laboratory in 1950 and has only recently retired, though he has meanwhile undertaken other duties. From 1954 to 1957 he was an expert with the FAO fisheries project in Ecuador. He served in the Faroese Administration from 1963 to 1967, and was elected a member of the Faroese Parliament, 1966-70.

An editor of the Faroese literary magazine *Varðin* since 1961, he is also a member of the Faroese Academy and former Chairman of the Faroese Authors' Society. Recently he read his poetry at poetry gatherings and on tour in Norway, and he has assisted the Nynorsk poet, Knut Ødegård, in compiling an anthology of Ødegård's translations of Faroese poems into Nynorsk. In February 1977, he represented the Faroese writers at the first Congress of the European Writers' Organisation and presented a short paper in support of translating Nordic literature. He has given unstinting and disinterested help in the preparation and editing of this present anthology of Faroese poetry in English translation.

His collections of poetry are: *Myrkrið reyða* (The Red Darkness), 1964; *Syngjandi grót* (Singing Stones), 1951; *Vatnið og ljósið* (Water and Light), 1960; and a selection of his poems, *Teinur og tal* (The Distance Travelled, and Talk), 1972. He has also published a book of short stories, *Leika-pettið* (Shards), 1971

In addition, he composed the texts of two anthems, which were performed at the openings of the Grammar School and the Art Gallery in Tórshavn, dated 1966 and 1977, respectively. Among his translations are poems from English, Spanish, Nynorsk, and Icelandic; a collection of his translations from Icelandic and Nynorsk was published in 1977 under the title *Frændarøddir* (Voices of Kinfolk). His edition of a selection of poems by the Faroese poet J.H.O. Djurhuus was published in 1961.

His own poetry and prose have been translated into English, Danish, Norwegian (including Nynorsk), Icelandic, Serbo-Croatian, and Brazilian Portuguese. An English translation of one of his stories is included in Hedin Brønner's *Faroese Short Stories,* published by The Library of Scandinavian Literature, 1972. See the Selected Bibliography for further details on this last-named publication.

WHITE SAND

Children, we went to the flat strand
long summer days
and played with the white sand.

Played with the great still heaps,
dear grains and shell riches
wave-borne from murky depths.

At times a grown awareness dawned
that my mind and world
were as the riddle-dark sea floor
and that my thoughts were waves
against headlands broken
and not on the flat strand.

One glittering second against the dark cliff
and then into the deep
my treasure of white sand rained.

OUT FROM THE ROCKY SHORE

Out from the rocky shore
I row my little boat
early in the morning —
prow straight to the sun's flaming wheel
— mightily it rolls up out of the sea rim,
warms me on the back,
spreads gold and red over the slopes and fells.
Birds sing, the sea plays over the oar-blades.
Ah, blessed sun —
I watch your green work
that shines from my house up on shore. —
You pour glitter on the sea,
make the hairs on the back of my hand live like grass,
— and deep under the boat
where my eyes cannot reach
your light sits below in the gleaming eyes of fish,
over and under me you make warmth and life —
and in me, who row over the deep
you make bright suns
to light my path, both outward and homeward.

DEW

Still seas,
the world wide and silent,
feelings come in to me by ways
as secret as those that wind and dew follow. —

Feelings, where do they come from?
suddenly they waken, grow warm and break into flame,
live like northern lights in lofty skies. —

The time has come to be still,
still and patient as grass, that stands in the fields and waits,
for a breeze that comes with refreshing dew
in from the wide seas.

THE DROP

Out of clear summer a shower fell
and on my forehead the first raindrop broke,
my heart turned to dew and my eyes to light,
my mind filled with life, as a quickening yolk.

Little token from space, clear and bright,
loosed a moment from water's mighty hand,
come by way of sea and the wide air,
kindle daylight and life along my strand.

Particles on our transient Earthly ways
we met, and all became bright and fiery;
my soul blazed like a crystal in the sun
and in me sang water springs and the sea.

WHITE NIGHT

A light begins to glow
— as though prisoned in the hills —
the wise men chafe to be going,
to journey across the bare fells.

White and indistinct night,
the world waits in stillness,
its arch frigid in the radiance
as the moon glimmers on the sea . . .

Suddenly tower from the glow
trunks of giant growth,
carry into the high air
wavelets of gray leaves.

The world is as though fraught
with bodings of salvation —
full of wonder the wise ones
go under the gray leaves.

Light lingers in the ashes,
the wise men sink to their knees,
praise be to the light's splendour
cascading from the white night . . .

Leaves tremble in the whirlwind,
shadows quicken on the hills, —
safe sleep the mother and baby
deep under the still ashes.

STONES

In my mother's hand stones glistened
that she had gathered from clean river gravel —
she reached green stones and blue towards me
and sparkling-quartz, clear as water.

Mother paid attention to stones,
she looked for the sea's green and the sky's blue in pebbles,
and great gray stones along the way
were living creatures to her.

When day and twilight mingle on slope and house
the summer night picks out the drab boulders, —
beautiful new-found songs take the rocky ridges
that glimmer too with the fairest stones.

REFLECTION

Sitting by your sickbed
I see the brightness of the sun
on the grass along the road
we walked so many times —
I see the rock-fast pylon,
poles that carry bright wires
firmly to the top of the hill
and out of sight.

I see grass stems ripple in the summer breeze.

Outside are the voices of children.
You ask me to raise the window.

Old friend of mine!
Can you not bear the glass
between you and the day
you and the children
and life
and the sea
beginningless endless sea
that we glimpse far beyond the children?

So neat, white and clean
around your pale face —
bright as the summer morning on the beach,
Sunday morning, we played with shells
dead calm on the strand
the sand bright and still.

Our ways parted when we were young,
ships took you far and wide,
your eyes grew old on the sea paths
and stories you could tell!

Long ago are the days
when we ran from the biggest waves,
surf up in the grass. —

Long ago are the winter mornings:
low sun flamed in on the beach,
bridges of driftwood,
bird tracks in the sand. —

TO RUTH

The land lived
scored into your eyes
painful and sorrow-burdened —
abrupt slopes
blinded by dead grass colour
fronted the steel-gray deep.

Cliff falls, the dark houses, rock sheer:
this ominous world
awed your sequestered soul
fearful — always fearful.

Your restless hands
tried to tame it in pictures:
the desolate-seeming land
giving way to the sea
to the overwhelming loneliness —
your restless hands drew it
as it looked from your face.

Yet one summer morning the land
— after a wakeful night —
was brighter than you could draw:
sun-clad steeps
unimaginably fair
greener than mown grass
greener than all that green
you have dreamed about some time —
sea heaving blue.

Suddenly loosed and leaped,
as though your world had splintered,
scattered like ashes
in the too-bright wildering splendour —
then might your eyes dazzle,
your weary hands give over.

BEDROCK

Fair as morning red
molten in fusing fire
you burst from the guts of earth —
air quivered with life in your heat,
in the sea's mirror your coming flamed,
you became the firm ground of my land. —
When the fire's roar was spent
you were deep unmoved stillness.
You! Clean-edged lichen-grown bedrock!

In summer gloaming like a bride
you send forth gleams,
your face brightens and fades
— crowned by the last of day —
you turn your hidden look to me,
hold me with life's riddle:
whence came we, where does the way lead hence?
At the end of a long path, here
we meet in summer gloaming. —
Asking and motionless you stare at me.
My tongue loosens in your stillness.

What do I know of myself
or of your locked face
mirrored in my stone-gray brain?
So near that my hand rests on you
you are yet remote as the stars,
far off as my children, my nearest and best-known,
far as my all, my thought knows nothing of myself,
all fades, mirrored in time's dark flood.

Even so, I feel your nearness
as a joy in my blood
that binds us together —
roundabout we can see it lead us
from the beginning up, and back to the beginning again.

Long before there was earth and growth here
ages washed over you
water and wind sang greetings to you.
I do not hold myself from time and stillness, quiet and age,
have not forgotten to listen when all is still,
the words stone-still, stone-dead do not frighten me,
for I sense a soul in your stillness,
life moves in you, and longing,
you too are in company with us,
changing and shaping as you go
to wordless dust, which is earth,
living dust, which is earth.

REGIN DAHL was born in Tórshavn in 1918. He studied literature in Denmark and has spent his adult life there, first as a reader with Wivels, publishers, and now with Gyldendal.

He has published six volumes of poetry:*Í útlegd* (In Exile), 1937; *Tokkaljóð* (Love Poems), 1944; *Beltisgyrði* (A Bird-catcher's Belt, in which he carries his catch), 1949; *Óttakvaeði* (Matins), 1955; *Gongubitar* (Snacks for the Road), 1965; and *Sneisaboð* (Errand without Importance), 1970. The last named is a selection, in which his own translations of his poems into Danish are printed alongside the Faroese. His most recent collection of poems, *Ordkumler/Orðakumlar* (Word-Cairns, in Danish and Faroese), appeared in 1978.

Other works of his are a book of aphorisms, *Leysasøkk* (Loosestones, used to drive whales in a whale hunt), 1944; and three anthologies: *Barnasangbók* (Songbook for Children), 1943; *Gevið brøður* (Listen, Friends), 1943; and *Veitslugávan* (Feast Gift), 1969. He has also written songs and made two records of these.

EARLY SPRING

Now comes the time again
when light breaks out of its shell —
and birds from the south drop down
from high heaven
like a shout of joy.

And I, with death's weight
on my bones and heart
with half-snuffed winter heart
I stare back at the sun
and laugh with wonder like a fool.

AN INTERVAL

A wonder in my hands:
middle and thigh
marigold-smooth —
and close to my ear
your voice buxomly
ecstatically muttering.

Eyes shut,
nostrils quivering
and mouth open
until I close it
until we close
again in a hard grip.

A wonder in my hands:
trunk and turned hip —
and sea scent
and roar
unceasing, unceasing.

FALL EVENING IN TÓRSHAVN

Through this narrow lane
we went on in the dusk
while the blue turf smoke
swam between the dark houses,
and the sounds of dusk-scared children
and scolding mothers
far off and near
came like waves
of quick music —
this was our world,
it was good to love here
and then grow old,
totter
cane in hand
up the steep slopes
under the frost-bright waxing moon.

MIDDLE-AGED WOMAN

And so in the evening he takes me;
often pretty drunk
and rough —
I pray God give me patience
and him pleasure;
then he is tired out
and like a sad little boy —
and I hug him
so he can go to sleep.
Then I pray God
that the one who will quicken from this
may not be twisted
like poor Christopher
nor half-witted like little Malena.
In Jesus' name: amen.

A COIN FROM CNOSSOS

A piece of currency in my hand
— and ancient times flash from my palm:
morning waves along the marble strand,
sun towns awake, gods greet
the whale spear and waving grain.

ALONG THE COAST

We sail along the coast
amid coal-smoke and the rising sun —
it is a long stretch
out from the clay banks,
wooded slopes and dust-red plough-lands.

The land is rich,
out on the deep-blue sound
white boats, over-loaded —
above them, northward,
hurrying barnacle geese.

We sail along the coast
in sunsmoke and spring stench —
and the child you gave me
from your dear loins
sits at the rail and sings.

A FACE ON SHIP-BOARD

At the rail you stood
and stared —
lips bitter, unkissed,
eyes empty as a washcloth,
down from your nostrils
lines of sleeplessness,
and by your chin
furrows of rejected love:
— love which tried,
offered itself,
and was rejected —
there has not often been a face
so oppressingly beautiful,
as yours when you stared long
brown-eyed
out into death's deeps.

SHROVE TUESDAY

Foreshore all melted marsh, hard going —
in golden air sea-birds wheeling and mewling.

A sunk barge is moored to a rotten head
where herring gulls perch and tear at the sea-weed.

In rushy under-brush is bustle and throng —
the company of small birds bursting with song.

Ice particles glitter like glassy specks —
every eye of water has its pair of ducks.

These blinding tears are not grief's thing,
they are cold wind and sun. It is spring.

STEINBJØRN B. JACOBSEN was born in Sandvík, a village on the southermost island, Suðuroy, in 1937. He has been a seaman and took a degree in education, in 1963. Since 1970 he has been Principal of the Faroese Folk High School. He has written two plays and two radio dramas.

His three collections of poetry are: *Heimkoma* (Homecoming), 1966; *Frœ* (Seeds),1968; and *Kjökr* (Disturbed Waters), 1976. He has published the following children's books: *Hønan og hanin* (Cock and Hens), 1970; *Mœið* (The Lamb), 1972; *Krákuungarnir* (Young Crows), 1972; *Gráisteinur* (The Gray Stone), 1975; and *Hin reyða ryssan* (The Red Horse), 1979. His volume of short stories, *Á veg millum bygda* (On the Road between Villages), was published in 1975. With Heðin M. Klein he collaborated on an anthology of European and American poems translated into Faroese, *Flytifuglar* (Migratory Birds), 1972.

His prose and poetry have been translated into English, Norwegian (and Nynorsk), Danish, Swedish, Serbo-Croatian, Czech, French, and Icelandic.

BLUE

Sky and sea
meet on the blue
horizon
those black cliffs are blue
the fells
the grass-green steeps.
are hazy with blue
sometimes.

(UNTITLED)

Wind
on
window
on
glass
and
eye
rain.

SUN BAIT

Sun on
sand bed

sole
sucking
sunwater a

small coalfish
swims in
sunsea

strikes at the
sun
swallows the
sun fly.

SEAFOWL AND SEA

My days as a child
come back to me:
seafowl and sea,
its perfect shape
likeness to the sea.

Morning after child's morning
endless, unintelligible sea,
sea's everlasting living shape
boundary with boundary changes.

And winter morning
sky and sea
whirling oneness
against the seafowl.

Driven you came
crying,
your wings were stiff
crying
plunging at times
yet proudly
towards the white shore.

Summer morning
at one with the sea;
winter morning
very oneness.

But you were always
a living thing,
horizon's child,
a sea image.

YOLK

Afloat on the sea
past midnight
I call up the suns
as eggs out of a bird.

Out from the deep the yolk
then the white
and the shell.

A SUMMER MOMENT

Marigolds in the ditch
walk on green stems
alongside us
under the blue sky:
we shall make whistles
with those stems.

ONLY SHOW ME

Only show me
only be
as you are
only show me
let me see
into the you
we all want to know
the peaceful
that is above
and in the deep
what the sea itself is
when all else
is only wind
and waves on the sea.

WE TWO

Your hair
shines in its blackness
bright sunshine
in haying weather
a waterfall of black
your teeth
flint veins
snow drifts
cascade colours
your mouth
redstone
evening red
a warmth
a living being
eyes
tarn beds
openings inwards
outwards
the first deep
are you
green grass
tickling straw
green grass
coolness rising
are you
white falls
fine-weather rain
white falls
mixing coolly

in the white falls
you springs peering
through green grass
you.

GIRL

(painting by Ingalvur av Reyni)
Under the yellow sun
on ruddy legs
clothed in waves
bright-coloured in the dawn
that splash around your islands
girl

WE WERE TOGETHER

First there was silence between us
then we began to talk
warily
peace came in our eyes
a marigold opened
before us
another folded itself around us
a strong bear began in my feet
I danced it before
your smiling face
in a peacefulness
that slowly came toward me
and carried the beat in its hands
we were together a long while
made naked to one another
clothed in a haze
within a peace that was living
a true peace.

GUÐRIÐ HELMSDAL was born in Tórshavn in 1941. Here she lived for 12 years and then went to Copenhagen. A graduate nurse, she is now a part-time medical secretary and a housewife with two young children, living in Leynar.

She has published two collections of poetry, each containing some poems in Faroese and some in Danish: *Lýtt lot* (Mild Breeze), 1963, and *Morgun í mars* (Morning in March), 1971. She has also written literary criticism for *Varðin*.

Her poetry has been translated into English, Danish, German, Nynorsk, French, Swedish, Serbo-Croatian, and Icelandic.

THIS EVENING

The roof is whiskery
like a man's beard
fresh fallen snow on the house
this evening under
the glowing vault
smoke hangs
on the snow-clad roof ridge.

This evening under
the blue vault
the snow is clean
as light
and the air fills
with child voices
in singing games.

Approach the house
in the sunset
you will hear music
it is not too much to say
you have never heard
so sweet a song
as the icicles sing
under the roof.

LOOSED COLD

Still, still
the mountains rise behind
red-blue in the gray
the cold is loosed
has waved itself off from the landscape
which now lies softening.

WAITING

From the fields I have
gathered flowers
into my room's
longing.

I have lit the candle
and the flowers breathe
I am waiting
till my beloved comes home.

The sparkling candle-light,
among the flowers
speechless colours
shortens my waiting.

TWO DAYS OUT

Wide, blithe
cruel, fierce
breathing, heaving
huge ocean.

Clean, clear, single:
birds and ocean
ocean and birds.

Burning sun
and quiet raindrops
that break on the sea.

Beginning, end
ocean, sky
and one ship on the ocean.

MEETING

Your hand without delay
sought mine
our meeting was wordless
but in our palms'
dark hollow
it sang
like the conch's distant roar.

FRIGHTENED PALE GIRLS

Frightened pale girls
go out in the night
pale questioning girls
all in the solitary night.

Grieving, all the girls
say good-bye in this night.
Questioning girls' eyes
twinkle like stars in the night.

CHERRY TREES & MAPLES

I remember again the colours
cherry tree
and maple
clearest bright red
full-sounding crescendo
of quivering reds

I dream a red-blue curtain
and colours outdoors
of autumn which played its insistent
last concert
to the red-blue curtain
and maple.

POETIC SELF-PORTRAIT

You
are the winds
that blow
the water
that runs in the river
shining Sirius
the moon.

You grew up in sea-spray
between day and night.

JOY IS YOUR NOTE

You are not the one
who will write
great, remarkable poems
about sorrow.

But joy is your note
in it you live,
joy, that like Sirius,
blazes in the night,
that is love.

Renewed from moment to moment.

———————————

Now spring breaks out
the city's year
come back again.

Erantis brings gold out of the frosthard earth
toddlers hop and skip on the cobbles.

Stones and streets
lived in year after year.

Every spring the way becomes longer
to the wide skies
of homeland and the sea.

But all at once it means nothing
because the pearl,
childhood's golden pearl

that turned the scale of the years
still clings like a limpet
where she belongs
while time sets his annulars
on her shell
first one, then another,
they number themselves
like ribbed sand.

STORM

I cannot sleep
for the wind behind my window
that shuts me in
alone with my longing.

It roars like the surf
when it breaks
and turns to foam.

If only it were a wave
that could carry me
to what I long for
out there in the night.

RÓI PATURSSON was born in Tórshavn in 1947. He has worked as a labourer in Tórshavn and in Denmark, and his poems, stories, and articles on various subjects have appeared in journals and newspapers.

He has published two small collections of verse, the first without title or date; the second was published in 1976 and is called *á alfaravegi* (on the public highway). He gives his name on this book as Rói Reynagarð Patursson.

THE TOWN
(and advertisements in the windows)

These dead pictures
in the windows
came to life
as I passed by
their eyes followed me.

I stopped
and heard footsteps in the evening
as I did yesterday
and shall tomorrow.
A thousand blind men
from factories and offices
glum and weary
sway before the pictures
in the windows
which criticise and tempt.

The body
became a stooped man
when the houses
with empty eyes
reached over the streets,
echoed the shoe scufflings
between them.

Then cars
and cars and again cars
of cold iron
chewed up the evening

and pushed my cheek
in against the windows,
then I was afraid,
gone wild between the houses,
I was an advertisement,
a car or a blind man.

Like a lonely
fluttering candle
on the planet.

DRUNK

Curiosity and thought
were thrust into the deep
by silence and you all.

I went
like a caged beast
along a stony, high wall
and searched.
I knocked uselessly
till my will and hand were broken,
I wanted out
but where was the hidden way?

I found it,
it was a small lie
that God too and all good were in on.

It brought the planets
and endless space
to life,
it quickened slowly,
no flame
just embers
and a red glow from the rest.
In the distant hum
from the planets
you all vanished
an overbig nothingness
was born again as music,

sounded for a moment
and faded away
to a man
who mournfully sat prisoner
of silence and you all.

But the hidden way
lures into space
where longing just grows
because freedom is unknown.

FLOWERPOWER

Wipe the drunkenness from your eyes.
Seek and you shall find.
Listen to the music of the river,
know life in the midst of the traffic,
think, listen, and enjoy yourselves.

Go with water and wind,
flower petals and sun.

But you must not lose your wits
and fall stoned among the flowers
because then the flowers will wither,
and the music will fade away
into the town roar.

And
the day you wake up
with shaking hands
and fumble after the tunes that have gone silent,
then your children will go after them,
and their feet will bleed.
Because the tunes have become sharp
as a million
broken bottles.

88

PLAY HIDE AND SEEK, GIRL
(Give a sign, girl!)

Big-eyed girl
I am afraid of you.
You play
you wave and smile
at everyone.
When you ask something
you tilt your head
with short words
you blink with your eyes
and look with your body.

But when I get near
you dry up inside
and talk . . .

You made me crazy.
Not because
I did not like you
but you brought doubt
in my love
for myself.

RHYTHM AND THE GIRL

She was in town.
And the houses came to life
in the rhythm
of her hips.

She was clear music,
a flaming naked dancer,
an Indian world
with rhythm
and bass-sitar.

She stopped.
And the sunshine burned
and waited
in the streets.

I felt empty,
she was away
and I knew nothing.

But her rhythms
were in space,
in my clothes.

They crept into my body
where they wake and tremble
every time
a girl passes.

ALEXANDUR KRISTIANSEN was born in Fuglafjørður, a village on the second largest island, Eysturoy, in 1949. He studied at the Teachers' College in Tórshavn and is now a teacher in his native village.

He has adapted stories for radio and published six collections of poetry: *Nón* (Mid-afternoon), 1968; *Assa* (a proper name), 1969; *Við fjøll og bláan fjørð* (By Fell and Blue Firth), 1972; *Jomfrú við ongum bróstum* (Virgin with No Breasts), 1972; *Málið er mítt øki* (Speech Is My Space), 1975; and *Várt dagliga lív* (Our Daily Life), 1979.

He has also published a songbook with music for children called *Kannubjøllivísir* (Horses-tails, i.e., *Equisetum*, the Latin botantical name for the weed horsestails), 1977.

His poems have been translated into English, Danish, Nynorsk, Icelandic, Swedish, and Serbo-Croatian.

WHAT IT IS TO BE A WINDOW

I am a window
I let folk look
out through me
and in through me
I reflect light back
but I also
take on: light, inspection,
rain, I do like rain
it scours me clean
and shiny
so I almost get
a crack in me
I do like to be a window
I do like it that folk
can see each other as they do
through me.

A POEM ABOUT SEA AND STARS

I shall come to you in the sea
I shall listen for you in the sea
I shall hear your laughter in the sea
see you smile in the sea
I shall kiss your face in the sea
I shall come to you in the sea
that I may die
in your salt embrace

tell me
why do stars and the marsh-lights shine?

TOES

I walked into the pasture — barefoot —
and counted my toes.
And while I walked this way, only
walked, 1 — 2 — 3, 1 — 2 — 3, it
was no longer I, but the toes
that walked, and I laughed at them,
and while they walked this way, and
I laughed at them, it was no
longer toes, but I, that walked, and
they laughed at me, that only walked in
the pasture barefoot and counted toes.

TO BE A TREE

to be a tree
in one's own
garden
to stand
out in front of
one's own window
and grow
with jubilant
heart
with bark for skin

to think of one's roots
that hold one fast
and will not let go

look alive
with many branches
and green leaves
and marks
of a thousand
bird claws

to stand there
straight and proud
out in front of
one's own window
and live one's own life.

TEXTS

silent we sat and heard life cautiously knocking
at our souls and shoeless we crept away through
the dark and knocked on all the doors in the
village empty and meaningless our shoes stay
behind

o

who hears my song in the ice-cold cluster of houses?
people behave as though I had opened a window.

o

it is not the beloved that warms your colours for you
soft flesh will wither in my hands like
a secret a wish

o

naked we were made and naked we want to
love one another

o

yolk so big that I can well believe in a dwelling
in which the white boils out as though it had never
seen by daylight my body your body as though
no line between just as there is no line between
blood and yolk.

SUMMER MORNING or GIRL IN A BIKINI

wet paper
and a landscape
of smelly
sea-weed
birds write
with bloody beaks
tracks in the sand

blue-green sea
gray paper
sea-weed
and wind
oily sea
rust-red eye-holes
in tide rock.

the bird drops
its feathers
your feet
stand out in
the water
bird-eyed
and your marvellous
little navel
that looks so
wonderfully at me

you smell of sea-weed
your body is salt

your hair is oil
your eyes are blood
footprints
nothing left
paper is white.

I MET YOU

I met you
you had vanished a long while
when I turned toward you
it was perhaps
nevertheless not you
thought I
and went away
and yet
perhaps we shall meet again.

ADVENT

the girl I met
was dark as a forest
deep as a forest
mysterious as a forest
and snowflakes fell
among the trees —

WITH CLOSED EYES

with closed eyes
he let the current
take over
the current carried him
far out to sea
where he at last
opened his eyes
and went his way.

HOMECOMING

at last he went
past the church
along the straight path
through the dale
to the village
where the houses stood
and was home.

STONES

stones and other things
live like sculptures
between words

in the beginning was the word
or the strand

STRAW

Straw
see this hill
squelch underfoot
nothing much to say
about peaks
surf on the foreshore
fog land
glimpsed

well-known places
ebb in the weeds
balance in the memory
like straws in the wind
like straws
when the boat overturns.

HEÐIN M. KLEIN was born in Gjógv, a village at the north end of Eysturoy, in 1950. He is now a teacher in the village of Sand on Sandoy.

He has written articles of literary cricitism for *Varðin*, and published one collection of poems, *Væmingar og vaggandi gjálv* (Tide Coming and Rolling Sea), 1969. He collaborated with Steinbjørn B. Jacobsen in preparing the anthology of poems in translation, *Flytifuglar* (Migratory Birds), 1972.

His poems have been translated into English, Danish, Nynorsk, Swedish, and Serbo-Croatian.

ONCE

Towards evening
we often cast off
from the pier's end
and sailed to Greenland
in two minutes.

A barnacled rock
hedged with sea-weed
once it was
our splendid ship.

Ah yes
once the sea broke
over our decks
then what fun
to be a man:
solemn and wise
pacing decisively
frowning
in sea boots
on the spray-wet decks —
you chawed
and made a long spit.

Our fisherman's luck
never gave out
in one haul
we filled the ship.

Then home we sailed
we hailed
Jacob B.
seaman's talk
was high and strong
angry and hard
we sighed
and | swore sometime
because that
was how it should be.

And down by the boathouse
the little women
small boned
no breasts yet
waving
smudgy kerchiefs
they greeted us
welcome back home.

AT ÁARVEG

30 July 1969 (4.15 a.m.)
mighty gulps
and complicated steps
a few drops among folks —
watch-works
the time

perhaps wound up:
feathers
outstretched
a gleeful noise
at the hour-hand
delighted
stands and crows. —
or else:
rhythm's gone wrong
off beat
hiccuping:
lay me down on the pavement.
poor chap
— who is around
to wind you up?

the last second
in line
with the hour hand
goes to sleep yawning
in its stumbling:
stop.

LOVE

sometimes:
a contest
— never a game
even less a memory:
a painless sigh.

but:
shaking and embracing
worship
refusal
a quivering roar
while the heart sings
in mournful torment
— repeated
over and over.

SHY HOPES

I stand and stare
at the rush-filled ditch
at the brooks
marigolds
sadly sighing
and yet smiling
towards me

and the vision grows
around me
and in me
crumbles and gathers
in shy hopes
and trembling delight

QUICKENING

colour and light
forthcoming
day after day
in the stillness' pleasure
grass that grows
and greens
daisies
and marigolds
a freshening breath
of new life

free-hearted sounds
from shore and hid brook
gathering strength
take shape and fullness
in the sweet peace

sea and sky
weave together
a blue oneness
the sea's
deep colour
brightens and clears
in the unkenned
nothing.

EMPTINESS

a dry taste
of cigarette
a single sound:
on my own feet
I go
nowhere
a sense
of shut space

suddenly
as though at unawares
a gloomy ray
takes
my glum face

then I fled
troubled
into the shadows
that grin with their teeth
along with me.

A GREETING

girl!
your lips
the bend of your hips
your embrace:
my moment's solidarity
and highest harmony
with myself
the whole world.

NOTES ON THE POEMS

Page 4: Christian Matras, 'Now Is Our Life like a Lantern Light':
Firth: a narrow arm of the sea; also, the opening of a river into the sea.

Page 5: Christian Matras, ' The Sheltering Wall ':   Skerry: a rocky isle; a reef.

Page 6: Christian Matras, 'Vithoy':
The name of the northermost island of the Faroes, which this poem is about, is Viðoy. The 'ð', historically, would have been pronounced as it is spelled here in English, but in modern Faroese it is not pronounced in this phonetic environment at all. Viðoy is pronounced 'vee-oy', but this seemed an impossible title for a poem. The Danish name for the island is Viderö, which is no better.
Scree: a pebble; a stone; also, a heap of stones or débris.
Dear freight: almost a technical term, meaning human 'freight' as distinguished from anything else on board. The Faroese is *hin dýri farmur*. See also the last line of the fourth stanza of 'Knee-Rocking Song', p.9.

Page 8: Christian Matras, 'Weather Troll':
In Norse mythology and folk-lore, a troll is a supernatural being, conceived sometimes as a dwarf, sometimes as a giant, fabled to inhabit caves, hills, and similar places. In popular superstition trolls are blamed when things go wrong, and for natural calamities and bad weather. According to the poet, 'Weather Troll' was inspired by an unusually dense fog that he experienced in Copenhagen.
Cards batt: the troll is supposed to be combing out and preparing a mass of cotton fibres (batt) for spinning.
She was too old: in Norse folk-lore the moon is masculine and the sun feminine.
Airts: points of the compass; directions.

Page 9: Christian Matras, 'Knee-Rocking Song':

Ness: a promontory; cape; headland.

Wrapped bottles: the Faroese word, *hosum*, is untranslatable as a single word in English; it means a glass bottle around which a wrapping has been knitted, in wool, like a sock. These bottle coverings are intricately patterned, and the knitting of them is an art.

Gaffer: old man, oldster.

Ghylls: ravines; also, brooks. See also 'Milk Women', p. 11.

Page 10: Christian Matras, 'Milk Women':
Leaze: pasture or grassland; meadow.

Page 25: William Heinesen, 'A Summer's Day':
Ranunculus: any of a large genus of herbs, the crowfoot.

Page 44: Karsten Hoydal, 'To Ruth':
The title refers to Ruth Smith (1913-1958), a Faroese artist, who became known as a talented illustrator as well as a landscape and figure (especially self-portrait) painter, and is now considered to have been one of the finest colourists in modern Faroese art.

Page 66: Steinbjørn B. Jacobsen, 'We Two':
Tarn: a small mountain lake or pool.

Page 71: Guðrið Helmsdal, 'This Evening':
The roof is whiskery: many older Faroese houses have grassy sodded roofs, and some new ones, too, are being built with the same kind of roofs for additional insulation.

Page 79: Guðrið Helmsdal, 'Joy Is Your Note':
Annulars: rings, as on a shell.

SELECTED BIBLIOGRAPHY

I. HISTORICAL AND OTHER DESCRIPTIONS OF THE FAROE ISLANDS:

⁓1. Annandale, Nelson. *The Faroes and Iceland: studies in island life.* Oxford, at the Clarendon Press, 1905. With 24 illustrations.

2. *Danish Journal*, The Faroe Islands, Special Edition. Copenhagen: Danish Ministry of Foreign Affairs, 1971. Seven authoritative articles with excellent photographs.

⁓3. *Faroe Isles Review.* Editor: Emil Thomsen. Published by Bókagarður, P.O. Box 160, Tórshavn, Faroe Islands. Five numbers to date. Articles, with colour photographs, on many aspects of the social, economic, and cultural life of the Faroes.

⁓4. Heinesen, William. *Føroyar, Gandaoyggjarnar; Faerøerne, de magiske Øer*; The Faroe Islands, the Magic Islands. Copenhagen: Rhodos, 1971. Texts in Faroese, Danish, and English, with about 100 full-page photographs by Gérard Franceschi.

5. Jacobsen, Jørgen-Frantz. *The Farthest Shore.* Translated from the Danish by Reginald Spink. Copenhagen: Danish Ministry of Foreign Affairs, 1965.

⁓6. Lindenskov, Kalmar, Alan Brockie, Petur Zachariassen, and Annfinnur Zachariassen, Editors. *Islands and People.* Tórshavn: Leikur, 1979. Parallel texts in Faroese, Danish and English, with black-and-white photographs, and comprehensive statistics on the country and its inhabitants.

7. Morris, William. Extracts from his 'Diary of a Journey to the Faroes and Iceland in 1871', published in *The Life of William Morris* by J.W. Mackail. London: Oxford University Press, 1950, pp.249-58.

8. Severin, Tim. 'The Sheep Islands', *The Brendan Voyage.*

London: Arrow Books, 1979, pp.94-121.

9. *The Sheep Letter.* Facsimile edition. Tórshavn, 1971. Parallel texts in Faroese, Danish, and English. English translation by Michael Barnes and David R. Margolin. With an introduction and a chronology of Faroese history and language development from 825 A.D. to 1970. This document is Duke Hákon Magnússon's special enactment for the Faroes, dealing with agricultural matters, dated 1298 A.D.

-10. West, John F. *Faroe: The Emergence of a Nation.* London: C. Hurst & Company; New York: Paul S. Eriksson, Inc., 1972. Traces '. . . the development of Faroe from a remote and insignificant Danish province into a nation with a constitutional and cultural life of its own.' Chapter VI discusses, among other things, 'the age of antiquarianism' (on the Faroese language and oral literary tradition), and 'the beginnings of Faroese literature'; and Chapter XII contains a sub-section of 'Faroese writers and artists'. Appendix E, English Bibliogrpahy, is the source, with the author's permission, of a number of the entries in this present Selected Bibliography.

-11. Williamson, Kenneth. *The Atlantic Islands: A Study of the Faroe Life and Scene.* With a Foreword by Eric Linklater. London: Collins, 1948. The second edition, 1970, has an extra chapter by Einar Kallsberg.

-12. Young, G.V.C. *From the Vikings to the Reformation: A Chronicle of the Faroe Islands up to 1538.* Douglas, Isle of Man: Shearwater Press, 1979.

II. THE FAROESE LANGUAGE AND LITERATURE:

-1. Hagström, Björn. 'The Faroese Language. Origin. Development. Status', *Faroe Isles Review*, Vol. 2, No. 1, 1977, pp.31-7.

2. Jakobsen, Jakob. 'Faröe. Remarks upon Faröese Literature

and History', *Saga-Book of the Viking Club*. London, January, 1905.

3. Lockwood, William B. *An Introduction to Modern Faroese*. Copenhagen, 1951.

4. _____The Language and Culture of the Faroe Islands', *Saga-Book*, Vol.13, part 4, 1952, pp.340-68. An account of the language, political situation, oral literature, and the need for Faroese philological studies.

5. Seymour-Smith, Martin. *Guide to Modern World Literature*, Vol.2. London: Hodder and Stoughton, 1975, p.379.

6. Thompson, Frank. 'Expanding the scope for Gaelic', *Books in Scotland*, No.3, Winter 1978-79. Compares the literary viability of Faroese and Gaelic to the advantage of the former.

III. THE FÆREYINGA SAGA IN ENGLISH TRANSLATION (FROM THE ORIGINAL ICELANDIC):

1. Johnston, George, translator. *The Faroe Islanders' Saga*. Oberon Press, 1975. Introduction by George Johnston, with Notes and Select Bibliography.

2. Press, Muriel, translator. *The Saga of the Faroe Islands*. London, 1934.

3. *The Tale of Thrond of Gate,* commonly called Færeyinga Saga, englished by F. York Powell. London: David Nutt, 270-71 Strand, 1896.

4. Young, G.V.C. and Cynthia R. Clewer, translators. *The Faeroese Saga*. Belfast, 1973. Freely translated with maps and genealogical tables.

IV. FAROESE POETRY IN ENGLISH TRANSLATION:

A. Folk-Songs and Ballads:

1. Borrow, George. *Works,* edited by Clement Shorter. London, 1923, Vol.8, pp.205-19. A translation of a Faroese ballad.

2. Carpenter, W.H. 'The Folk Songs of the Faroe Islands', *The New Englander,* Vol.41, May 1882, pp.406-13. A brief account of the state of the language at this date and of the ballad tradition. *Lokka táttur,* a ballad of 96 stanzas, is given in translation.

3. Kershaw, N. *Stories and Ballads of the Far Past.* Cambridge University Press, 1921, pp.178-216. Contains 'The Faroese Ballad of Nornagest' (pp.178-81); 'The Ballad of Hjalmar and Angantyr' (pp.184-5); 'The Ballad of Arngrim's Sons' (pp.196-211); and 'Gátu Ríma' (pp.212-16): each one with a melody.

4. Prior, R.C. Alexander. *Ancient Danish Ballads.* London and Edinburgh, 1860, Vol.1, pp.334-42. A translation of a short Faroese ballad.

5. Smith-Dampier, E.M., translator. *Sigurd the Dragon-Slayer. A Faroese Ballad Cycle.* Oxford, 1934. A translation of the most celebrated of the Faroese ballad cycles.

6. Smith-Dampier, N. 'The Song of Roland in the Faroes', *Saga-Book,* Vol.11, 1936, pp.239-46. An account of the arrival of the Roland legend in Faroe, with a translation of 26 stanzas of the Faroese ballad.

B. Lyric Poetry:

1. Djurhuus, Hans A. 'Summer-Night', *Fanfaroe,* The Faroe Islands Force Magazine, No.5, Christmas 1943, p.8.

2. Djurhuus, J.H.O. A few poems translated from the Faroese by Stephen Wilkinson and G.M. Gathorne-Hardy. *Saga-Book,* Vol.12, December 1945, pp.255-60.

3. _____. 'Tova', translated by Wayne O'Neil. *The American-Scandinavian Review.* Vol.LI, No.2 (June 1963),

p.182. A short poem on a Danish historical theme.

4. Heinesen, William. 'Rain in Leningrad', translated by George Johnston. *Poetry* (Chicago), Vol.116, Nos.5-6, August-September 1970.

5. _____. 'Winter Lights Its Flame on Our Mountains' translated by George Johnston. *Trends* (Scotland), Vol.3, No.5, 1980.

6. _____.'The Dark Talks to a Blossoming Bush', translated by George Johnston. *Trends* (Scotland), Vol.3, No.5, 1980.

7. _____. 'Stone Girl', translated by George Johnston. *Trends* (Scotland), Vol.3, No.5, 1980.

8. _____. 'A Summer's Day', translated by George Johnston. *Anthos* (Ottawa).

9. _____. *Arctis: Selected Poems, 1921-1972*, translated and with an Introduction by Anne Born. Stornoway, Isle of Lewis: The Thule Press, 1980.

10. Hoydal, Karsten. 'White Night', translated by George Johnston. *Poetry* (Chicago), Vol.116, Nos.5-6, August-September 1970.

11. _____. 'Stones', translated by George Johnston. *Poetry* (Chicago), Vol.116, Nos.5-6, August-September, 1970.

12. _____. 'To Ruth', translated by George Johnston. *Quarry* (Canada).

13. _____. 'White Sand', translated by George Johnston. *Quarry* (Canada).

14. _____. 'White Sand', translated by George Johnston. *Trends* (Scotland), Vol.3, No.5, 1980.

15. _____. 'Out from the Rocky Shore', translated

by George Johnston. *Trends* (Scotland), Vol.3, No.5, 1980.

16. _____. 'The Drop', translated by George Johnston. *Trends* (Scotland), Vol.3, No.5, 1980.

17. Jacobsen, Steinbjørn B. 'Sun Bait', translated by George Johnston. *Anthos* (Ottawa) .

18. _____. 'A Summer Moment', translated by George Johnston. *Inscape* (Ottawa).

19. _____. 'Yolk', translated by George Johnston. *Inscape* (Ottawa).

20. Matras, Christian. 'The Company of the Blind', translated by George Johnston. *Poetry* (Chicago), Vol.116, Nos.5-6, August-September 1970.

21. _____. 'So Deep, So Deep', translated by Goerge Johnston. *Poetry* (Chicago), Vol.116, Nos.5-6, August-September 1970.

22. _____. 'Milk Women', translated by George Johnston. *Anthos* (Ottawa) .

23. _____. 'The Sheltering Wall', translated by George Johnston. *Quarry* (Canada).

24. _____. 'Weather Troll', translated by George Johnston. *Quarry* (Canada).

25. _____. 'Far off the Sea', translated by George Johnston. *Tamarack Review* (Canada).

26. _____. 'Viðoy', *Fanfaroe,* The Faroe Islands Force Magazine, No.5, Christmas 1943, p.8.

27. _____. 'Vithoy', translated by George Johnston. *Trends* (Scotland), Vol.3, No.5, 1980.

28. _____. 'We Two on the Still Stand', translated by George Johnston. *Trends* (Scotland), Vol.3,

No.5, 1980.

29. _____. 'Now Is Our Life like a Lantern Light', translated by George Johnston. *Trends* (Scotland), Vol.3, No.5, 1980.

V. FAROESE PROSE IN ENGLISH TRANSLATION:

A. Novels:

1. Brú, Heðin. *The Old Man and his Sons,* translated from the Faroese and with an Introduction by John F. West. New York: Paul S. Eriksson, Inc., 1970.

2. Heinesen, William. *Niels Peter,* translated from the Danish by Ian Noble. London: George Routledge & Sons, Ltd., 1939.

3. _____. *The Lost Musicians,* translated from the Danish by Erik J. Friis, with an Introduction by Hedin Brønner. New York: Twayne Publishers, Inc., and The American-Scandinavian Foundation, 1972.

4. _____. *The Kingdom of the Earth,* translated from the Danish and with an Introduction by Hedin Brønner. New York: Twayne Publishers, Inc., 1974.

5. _____. *The Good Hope,* translated from the Danish by John F. West. Stornoway, Isle of Lewis: The Thule Press, 1981.

6. Jacobsen, Jørgen-Frantz. *Barbara,* translated from the Danish, and with a biographical note on the author, by Estrid Bannister. Harmondsworth, Middlesex: Penguin Books Ltd., 1948.

7. Thomsen, Richard B. *The Tyrants,* translated from the Danish by Naomi Walford. London, 1955; paperback edition, 1960.

B. Short Stories:

122

1. Brønner, Hedin, translator. *Faroese Short Stories*, with an Introduction and Notes by Hedin Brønner. New York: Twayne Publishers, Inc., and The American-Scandinavian Foundation, 1972. Twenty-five stories by eleven authors: M.A. Winther, Sverri Patursson, Hans Dalsgaard, William Heinesen, Hedin Brú, Martin Joensen, Valdemar Poulsen, Karsten Hoydal, and Jens Pauli Heinesen.

2. Brú, Hedin. 'Emanuel', translated from the Faroese by Hedin Brønner. *The American Scandinavian Review*, Vol.LV, No.2 (Summer 1967).

3. _____. 'Lice', translated from the Faroese by Hedin Brønner. *The American-Scandinavian Review*, Vol.LIX, No.2 (Summer 1971).

4. _____ 'Men of Letters', translated from the Faroese by Hedin Brønner. *The American-Scandinavian Review*, Vol.LIX, No.3 (Autumn 1971).

5. _____. 'Old Halgir', translated from the Faroese by Hedin Brønner. *The American-Scandinavian Review*, Vol.LVIII, No.2 (Summer 1970).

6. _____. 'Old Halgir', translated from the Faroese by Hedin Brønner. *Faroe Isles Review*, Vol.1, No.1, 1976, pp.20-22.

7. _____. 'The White Church', translated from the Faroese by Hedin Brønner. *The American-Scandinavian Review*, Vol.LIV, No.4 (Winter 1966-67).

8. Heinesen, William. 'Belsmand', translated from the Danish by Donald K. Watkins. *The American-Scandinavian Review*, Vol.LIX, No.4 (Winter 1971-72).

9. _____ . 'The Celestial Journey', translated from the Danish by Hedin Brønner. *The American-Scandinavian Review*, Vol.LIX, No.1 (Spring 1971).

10. Joensen, Martin. 'Shavings' (no translator given), *Faroe*

Isles Review, Vol.2, No.2, 1977, pp.38-40.

C. Folk-Tales and Legends:

1. Jakobsen, Jakob. 'Upsala-Pætur's Christmas', translated from the Faroese by Hedin Brønner. *The American-Scandinavian Review*, Vol.LVII, No.4 (December 1969).

2. _____.'The Legend of Snæbjörn', translated from the Faroese by John F. West. *Faroe Isles Review*, Vol.1., No.2, 1976, pp.12-15.

3. _____. 'The Seal Wife', translated from the Faroese by John F. West. *Faroe Isles Review*, Vol.3, No.1, 1978, pp.32-33.

4. _____. *Faroese Folk-Tales and Legends*, translated from the Faroese by John F. West.Lerwick,Shetland Islands: Shetland Publishing Co., 1980.

VI. **CRITICAL AND OTHER STUDIES OF FAROESE WRITERS AND LITERATURE:**

1. Brønner, Hedin. 'Heðin Brú: Faroese Novelist', *The American-Scandinavian Review*, Vol.LIX, No.4 (Winter 1971-72).

2. _____. 'Jørgen-Frantz Jacobsen and Barbara', *The American-Scandinavian Review*, Vol.LXI, No.1.

3. _____. 'William Heinesen: Faroese Voice — Danish Pen', *The American-Scandinavian Review*, Vol.LXI, No.2.

4. _____. *Three Faroese Novelists*. New York: Twayne Publishers, Inc., 1973. An appreciation of Jørgen-Frantz Jacobsen, William Heinesen, and Heðin Brú.

5. Conroy, Patricia. 'Sniolvs kvæði. The Growth of a Ballad Cycle', *Fróðskaparrit*, Vol.26, 1978, pp.33-55.

6. _____ . 'Ballad Composition in Faroese Heroic Tradition: the case of "Hernilds kvæði" ', *Fróðskaparrit*, Vol.27, 1979, pp.75-101.

124

7.   Foote, Peter G. 'On Legal Terms in *Færeyinga Saga*,' *Fróðskaparrit. Annales Societatis Scientiarum Faroenis*, X (Tórshavn, 1961), pp.47-52.

8.   _____. *On the Saga of the Faroe Islanders*. Text of a lecture delivered at University College, London, 12 November 1964.

9.   _____. 'Færeyinga saga, chapter forty', *Fróðskaparrit*, XII (1964), pp.84-98.

10. _____. 'brandr and the Apostles', *Medieval Literature and Civilization, Studies in Memory of G.N. Garmonsway*. London, 1969, pp.129-40.

11. _____. 'A Note on brandr's kredda', *Afmælisrit* Reykjavík: Jóns Helgasonar, 1969, pp.355-63.

12. _____. 'A Note on Some Personal Names in *Færeyinga Saga*', *Otium et Negotium, Studies in Onamatology and Library Science Presented to Olof von Feilitzen*, Stockholm, 1973.

13. Hátun, Ólavur. 'The ballad', *Faroe Isles Review*, Vol.2, No.2, 1977, pp.34-37.

14. Jones, W. Glyn. '*Noatun* and the Collective Novel', *Scandinavian Studies* (1969), pp.217-30. A study of William Heinesen's novel *Noatun*, translated as *Niels Peter*.

15. _____. 'William Heinesen and the Myth of Conflict', *Scandinavica* (1970), pp.81-94.

16. _____. *William Heinesen*. New York: Twayne Publishers, Inc., 1974. A critical study in Twayne's World Authors Series, TWAS 282, Denmark.

17. Ker, W.P. 'On the History of the Ballads 1100-1500', *Proceedings of the British Academy*, Vol.LV (1909), pp.179-205. A general survey containing much mention of Faroese ballads.

18. Nolsoe, Mortan. 'Our folk-ballads . . .', *Faroe Isles Review*, Vol.2, No.2, 1977, pp.29-33.

TITLES FROM WILFION BOOKS, PUBLISHERS

THE CONTEMPORARY POETS SERIES

Vol. 1. *Treason Has a Voice* by Konrad Hopkins
ISBN 0 905075 00 5
Hardcover: £1.00 U.K./$3.00 U.S.A./fl. 10 — Holland

Vol. 2. *Poems by Malin* by Nigel Malin
ISBN 0 905075 01 5
A RonKon Paperback: £0.50 U.K./$1.50 U.S.A./fl. 3. —
Holland

Vol. 3. *I, Aquarius: Poems for the New Age* by Ronald van
Roekel
ISBN 0 905075 03 X
A RonKon Paperback: £1.25 U.K./$3.00 U.S.A./fl. 8. —
Holland

Vol. 4. *Mona My Love and Other Manx Poems* by Michael
Daugherty
ISBN 0 905075 05 6
A RonKon Paperback: £1.25 U.K./$3.00 U.S.A./fl. 8. —
Holland
With an essay on 'The Isle of Man, Its Literature and
Language' by Margaret Killip.

Vol. 5. *Flowers in the Forest* by Henry Mair
ISBN 0 905075 07 2
A RonKon Paperback: £1.00 U.K./$2.50 U.S.A./fl. 6. —
Holland
With an essay on 'My Visit to the U.S.S.R., 1978' by
Henry Mair.

THE GENIUS OF THE LOW COUNTRIES SERIES

Vol. 1. *Quartet: An Anthology of Dutch and Flemish Poetry*
ISBN 0 905075 04 8
A RonKon Paperback: £2.50 U.K./$5.00 U.S.A./fl. 15. —
Holland

Forty poems by Judith Herzberg, Arie van den Berg, Patricia Lasoen, and Eddy van Vliet in English translation. With an 'Introduction' by Konrad Hopkins and Ronald van Roekel, biographical notes, and a selected bibliography.

THE RENFREWSHIRE MEN OF LETTERS SERIES

Vol. 1. *William Sharp/Fiona Macleod* by Konrad Hopkins and Ronald van Roekel
Renfrew District Libraries Paperback: 35p
A biographical sketch, with cover portrait, a selection of poetry and prose, and bibliographies.

Vol. 2. *John Wilson/Christopher North* by Konrad Hopkins and Ronald van Roekel
Renfrew District Libraries Paperback: 35p
A biographical sketch, with cover portrait, a selection of poetry and prose, and bibliographies.

THE SCOTLAND ALIVE SERIES

Vol. 1. *The Common Bond* by John Rodgers
ISBN 0 905075 11 0
A RonKon Paperback: £2.00 U.K./$5.00 U.S.A. and Canada/fl. 15. — Holland
A study of literary, biographical and historical associations between Scotland and America by a Kilbarchan poet-historian, with a 'Foreword' by Mary A. Rodgers.

AND

Cross Winds: An Anthology of Post-War Maltese Poetry
Compiled and with an introductory essay on Maltese
literature by Oliver Friggieri
ISBN 0 905075 08 0
A RonKon Paperback: £3.50 U.K./£M3.50 Malta/$7.00
U.S.A./fl. 20. — Holland
Fifty-two poems by twenty-one poets, in English, with
biographical notes, and a selected bibiliography.

The Wilfion Scripts by William Sharp/Fiona Macleod
Transmitted through the mediumship of Margo Williams
ISBN 0 905075 09 9
A RonKon Paperback: £3.00 U.K./$8.00 U.S.A./fl. 20. —
Holland
Ninety-two verses, two other poems, and an
autobiographical essay dictated by the Scottish man of
letters, William Sharp/Fiona Macleod ('Wilfion'), 1855-
1905, to the English medium Margo Williams, with an
'Introduction' by Konrad Hopkins and Ronald van
Roekel, a 'Conclusion' by Elizabeth A. Sharp, and 'Notes
on *The Wilfion Scripts*' by Walter Williams, Konrad
Hopkins and Ronald van Roekel.

Rocky Shores: An Anthology of Faroese Poetry
Compiled and translated by George Johnston
ISBN 0 905075 10 2
A RonKon Paperback: £4.00 U.K./$10.00 U.S.A. and
Canada/Kr. 48.00 Faroe Islands and Denmark/fl. 20. —
Holland
Nine poets, eighty-two poems, in English translation,
with an 'Introduction' by George Johnston, biographical
notes, and a selected bibliography. A title in the Unesco
Collection of Representative Works, European Series.